Committed Relationships

Revised Edition

QUAKERbooks

First published in July 2001 by Quaker Books, Friends House. Euston Road, London NWI 2BJ

Revised reprint March 2007

ISBN 0 85245 398 1

978 85245 398 8

Contents

Committed Relationships

My dear friends, let us love one another; because the source of love is God. Everyone who loves is a child of God and knows God, but the unloving know nothing of God; for God is love.

1 John 4.7-8

About this book

This handbook has been prepared in response to concerns expressed by many elders and overseers in Britain Yearly Meeting – and indeed, by many members and attenders – about changes in our culture and in society at large in the attitude to marriage and other committed relationships.

We have carefully explored the changes in attitude to marriage and other life-long committed relationships within our meetings. We have found light in dark places, both within and outside ourselves, and this has led us towards some questions, which form the structure of this new book. We are grateful to those who have already laid trails for us to follow, and to those who engaged in exploration alongside us. We hope that the questions raised in this handbook may lead to deeper consideration and a wider understanding of this issue in meetings.

We are all to take a 'right share in the privilege of watching over one another for good', as *Quaker faith & practice(Qfp)** 12.19 reminds us. Therefore in this book we understand 'elders' or 'overseers' to include all who undertake this responsibility seriously and with commitment, whether their meeting makes formal appointment or shares the tasks corporately.

What are the changes in British society?

Politicians may try to promote a return to the 'family values' of the past but the past was never perfect, and in contemporary British society, where one in three modern marriages ends in divorce within five years, we have to face reality. An increasing number of people now live alone. It is common for both men and women to work and have careers. Many couples now live together quite soon after they have met. Reliable contraception usually enables children to be planned for. Changes to the laws of inheritance and in the public's attitude to illegitimacy mean that some couples feel no need to marry, even if they have children together. At the same time, many couples are choosing to live together and many make a lifelong commitment. Since December 2005, civil partnership legislation has enabled same sex couples to register their civil partnership in a similar form to a civil marriage. This ceremony entitles the civil partners to the same legal,

---

* Details of this and other publications can be found in Appendix 5, Publications page 40

financial and inheritance rights and responsibilities as a married heterosexual couple (see Appendix 1).

Some people may regret the changes (perhaps comparing them critically with their own lives) and find them difficult, disturbing, even painful. Others may find them liberating, affirming and creative. Whatever our feelings may be, we must acknowledge that society's conventions are always changing and that Friends' lives change with them (see, for example, *Quaker faith & practice*, sections 22.33 and 23.46).

> Quaker difficulties can be resolved in Quakerly ways. When mountains of tradition block the path – whether they represent long habit, theological disagreement, inherent reserve, or simply new ideas – faith can move them. For Friends, faith is a movement. It leads from the One. To each one, to many. And from there, out towards the all. If Quakers are to live their witness, no part of that process is dispensable.
>
> Earlham School of Religion   1999

How are these changes reflected in our meetings?

It is sometimes said that the membership of our Society is getting older and that our meetings are rather backward-looking. But we do not believe this is wholly true. We try to encourage anyone who might be interested in Quaker ways to come and worship with us. Our meetings are made up of people of all ages, and from a variety of backgrounds, who live their lives in many different ways. Some people in our meetings live alone, either from choice or following widowhood or divorce. Some live with their parents or families; others live with their partners – some are married, some have long-term relationships, some have just started to live together.

What are committed relationships?

We have a wide and varied range of commitments in our lives. We have commitments to organisations – the company we work for, our Religious Society, the charitable organisations we support. And we have commitments to individuals – colleagues, clients, friends, members of our families. These vary in depth and length. Our religious convictions and our family relationships are likely to be enduring commitments. Many of these commitments may be within or brought to our meetings. However, in this handbook we focus on the specific commitment between two adults who have chosen to live together in an intimate and lifelong union, and on its outward recognition.

What is the role of the meeting in committed relationships?

Quaker faith & practice offers several examples of the role of the meeting in committed relationships:

> The meeting will only live if we develop a sense of community... If all those who belong to our meeting are lovingly cared for, the guidance of the Spirit will be a reality.
>
> *Qfp* 10.03

> We are aware of the need to care for ourselves and each other in our meetings, bearing each others' burdens and lovingly challenging each other.
>
> *Meeting for Sufferings 1992 Qfp* 29.02

Our meetings try to be communities which worship together and care for one another. We are aware of the need to acknowledge, value and support all those who have lovingly and freely chosen to weave the threads of their lives together, committing themselves to an undertaking which will both enrich and tax them as individuals and as a couple. As we try to find 'that of God in everyone' we might keep in mind William Penn's words in 1693:

> As love ought to bring them together, so it is the best way to keep them well together.
>
> *Qfp* 22.35

Committed Relationships

My partner and I decided we could not legally marry but were being led instead to have a 'celebration of commitment'.... What seemed essential for us was the public witnessing of a commitment made before God by one's worshipping community, who then also took a responsibility to uphold it.

Qfp 22.46

In order to grow, I need my church to bless and uphold not just me as an individual, but also our relationship.

Qfp 22.29

A meeting for worship for the solemnisation of marriage is held in the same form and spirit as a Friends' meeting for worship at other times. It is an occasion when the parties to the marriage may gain inspiration and help from the meeting, which may continue to be a source of strength to them during their married life.

Qfp 16.02

One Friend wrote that it is sometimes said of Friends that we are very clear about the things we do not believe but much less clear about what we do believe. Celebrating and affirming 'that of God' in ourselves and each other must surely mean that we celebrate and affirm the manifestation of that belief in loving and committed relationships, and accept the responsibility to encourage and sustain such relationships.

How do we help couples prepare for a committed relationship?

> Finding a true and faithful loving relationship may well be the greatest experience of our lives... Such relationships are, however, challenging as well as fulfilling, and the fulfilment does not come without the challenge. Tension can be either the source of learning and growth or the cause of hostility and the breakdown of relationships. Responding to the Holy Spirit, both individually and together, we may grow through problems and pain as well as shared joys and interests, and find deeper understanding.
>
> *Qfp* 22.47

We start learning about relationships from birth. We continue to learn from parents, family members, friends, relatives and colleagues. Literature, film and television, religion and culture often present idealised relationships. From all these experiences we create our own internal concept of the sort of committed, long-term relationship we would hope to make with another adult. We may be reacting against our own experiences of poor relationships or trying to recreate the happiness we grew up with. If we find a partner and live and grow together, the idealised image may become more grounded in reality. In all such intimate relationships, the possibility exists to be more safe or vulnerable, more creative or destructive than at any other time in our lives. With love, grace and hard work

11

by both partners, that process of growth and change can be maturing and enriching. Change, however much it is wished for and welcomed, is rarely accomplished without difficulty.

This process of growing into a relationship with another person can be eased and enriched by increasing self-awareness, by learning tolerance and perspective, by awareness of the process of change, and by the development of good communication. The process can be sustained and blessed by the loving spiritual support of individuals in the meeting and by the meeting as a whole. A meeting for clearness at an early stage can help the two people to explore their relationship as they consider making a life-long commitment.

As a worshipping community, truly believing in the centrality of love in our lives as a manifestation of 'that of God in everyone', we have a duly to nurture and uphold everyone in our meeting 'watching over one another for good' (*Qfp* 12.18-19). Couples who are committing themselves to living together will need our respect for their wishes in that choice, and our loving guidance. In accepting that duty, we, as Quakers, are acknowledging the growing spiritual, emotional and possibly physical aspects of the relationship. This responsibility may require us to challenge our own assumptions and expectations as well as those of the two people concerned, with sensitivity, love and clear-sightedness.

Until the 19th century, marriage in this country was very much a public affair – business-like rather than romantic; a matter of property, inheritance, family arrangement; a social institution. While this model had limitations, it offered a clear structure with well-defined roles and responsibilities. Couples today look primarily for a high degree of personal fulfilment within their relationship, yet have far fewer models, structures and skills to enable them to attain this.

We have a cloud of assumptions about 'being in love', about marriage, about long-term intimate relationships. Arising from these assumptions are expectations which may or may not be well founded in reality. Once a couple have decided to make a public avowal, it can be difficult for them to admit uncertainties and differences, to raise concerns: when all the emphasis is on looking forward, it may be hard to look back, to consider how they have come to be where they are, and to reflect on this in terms of a shared future. Yet such admissions and reflections are crucial to the continued well-being of the relationship. We should encourage couples who are considering making a public commitment to take the opportunity to stand back and make time for such discussion in the company of loving and supportive Friends.

Many subjects are hard to discuss at this stage – 'What happens when we fall out of being in love and move into loving?' (M. Scott Peck, 1990). Are the couple aware of strategies which will help them through the periods of

stress and difficulty that will arise in any relationship?
In our culture, the sexual relationship is often seen as
paramount. Because a couple are close and fulfilled
physically, there is often the assumption that this is the
rock on which to build their relationship, and that other
issues will sort themselves out naturally. Such perception
distorts the reality that close and satisfying physical
intimacy is only part of the whole. Close and satisfying
spiritual, emotional and intellectual intimacy are also
crucial if a relationship is to grow and endure.

The advice given to registering officers to meet with
applicants for marriage at a very early stage (*Qfp* 16:14)
might well be extended to any couple seeking to make a
public declaration of their commitment. Many meetings
do accept the suggestion that the registering officer 'may
find it an advantage to draw one or more other Friends
into these conversations'. To do so emphasises the fact
that, if a meeting is being asked to support a couple in
a committed relationship, it is important for the meeting
to feel confident that it has a realistic understanding of
that relationship. Such visits give an opportunity for the
representatives of the meeting and the couple to explore
this together in an open and upholding environment.

The couple need to be clear that the visit has real
meaning, that it is an opportunity to clarify the relationship
they are asking the meeting to support. The visitors need
to be clear that their visit has real purpose, that they are
not there to rubber-stamp the couple's request. Their

function is to clarify and honour the responsibility that the meeting is being asked to accept, in a prayerful and possibly challenging way. All present need to be open to the Spirit, listening to each other with grace and love.

However, we would rather encourage meetings to use the more reflective and structured format of a meeting for clearness (see page 16) which can be more enabling and on-going for the couple.

Where one of the couple does not come to meeting for worship, he or she should be encouraged to learn enough about Quakerism to be able to understand its importance to his or her partner, and the significance of the proposed meeting for commitment. When one or both of a couple move away from the current meeting, local overseers should ensure that they transfer responsibility for the couple's care to the overseers of the new meeting (see *Qfp* 16.52).

Couples wishing to marry in meeting receive advice on procedures from our registering officers. Some churches offer (or require couples to attend) marriage preparation courses but Quakers make no such provision. To our knowledge, no such courses are offered to those choosing a civil wedding or any couple making a commitment to live together. Organisations (see page 36) such as Relate offer couples courses which we recommend. The Association For Marriage Enrichment promotes Focus on Couples events which work at increasing the joy and reducing unhappiness for couples.

At present registration of civil partnerships cannot legally form part of a meeting for worship. Same sex couples can however celebrate their spiritual commitment to each other in a meeting for worship organised for that purpose (See *Qfp* 22.46).

Questions for reflection and discussion

1. How sensitive are we to those in our meeting embarking on such processes of change?

2. What do we offer couples preparing for a long-term committed relationship? Do meetings have the resources and the will to undertake such work?

3. How conscious is our meeting of the need to sustain those in committed relationships and how can this be done?

4. Under present circumstances, what might Friends do to support personally those same sex couples who would wish to celebrate both the legal and the spiritual dimensions of their relationship at the same time?

Meetings for clearness

It can be very difficult to discuss with relatives and friends, in an objective way, a wish to make a commitment to one another. When a couple announce that they are planning to marry or register their partnership, the prevailing and overwhelming response is usually so positive that any doubts may be trampled underfoot in the excitement of discussing the arrangements. One of the couple may have concerns but leave them unvoiced for fear of hurting anyone's feelings amid the outpourings of joy. Friends may be better able to consider the couple as individuals, and to ensure that both of them are clear about what they are proposing to do.

Within our Quaker tradition we have the practice of meetings for clearness. Originally introduced to ensure that persons planning to marry were 'clear' of any conflicting obligations, as suggested by *Quaker faith & practice* 16.19-21, they are increasingly being used to reflect on and explore the rightness of a decision. Sometimes meetings for clearness are suggested only when there is concern about the relationship. This is subjective and discriminatory. Some meetings have made a meeting for clearness part of their regular procedure for the preparation for marriage. We encourage all couples proposing to enter into a committed relationship to explore their decision in this way.

> The aim of such a meeting is to allow the couple to explore what their commitment will mean to them as they plan their future life together.
>
> *Qfp* 16.20

> Remember, the word is clearness, not clearance,
> implying that clarity rather than permission is sought.
>
> Peter Woodrow, 1994

Members of a committee for clearness need to be very
certain of their role – they are not meeting with the couple
as professional counsellors or therapists, neither are they
coming together as friends to talk over a problem and
give advice. They are meeting in confidence to enable the
couple to explore the nature of the commitment they are
contemplating, by acting as a channel for the guidance of
the Spirit.

> They are to listen without prejudice, to help clarify
> decisions and their implications, to facilitate
> communication where necessary, and to provide
> emotional support as an individual or family seeks to
> find God's will.
>
> New England Yearly Meeting, 1993

For such meetings to be of real and lasting value, the
couple should be helped to explore their commitment to
God, to one another and to the meeting. They will need
to look in depth at their own family's patterns, values
and relationships, and at the outcome of any previous
relationships or marriages; to consider their attitudes
towards the care of any existing or future children; where
and how they are going to live; their employment and
finance; and how they can make decisions about their
life together. Such prayerful reflections will require love,

sensitivity and self-awareness on the part of committee members, as well as the willingness to ask difficult questions, to explore unsafe areas, and to confront problematic issues in ways that are enabling to the couple.

Some of the approaches the group might use are:

- **Raising questions**

Not necessarily as direct challenges to the couple, but reframing and exploring issues differently – e.g. 'Have you considered the implications of......?'

- **Highlighting unchecked assumptions**

Sometimes couples feel compelled to move in directions which will fulfil other people's expectations (parents, relatives, friends, each other) without questioning or clarifying what those expectations are, or where they come from. Each may also be looking individually towards a personal vision or goal in the relationship which is not rooted in an understanding of themselves – their own needs and growth – or those of the other.

- **Acting as a mirror**

Reflecting back the implications of the proposed union, looking at possible areas of difficulty, identifying possible strategies and solutions, affirming the couple's areas of strength.

- **Modelling good communication**

Creating a safe and open environment in which feelings and concerns can be expressed. Ensuring that all present listen sensitively and non-judgmentally, refraining from pressing their own 'agenda' or emotions onto the couple.

- **Offering on-going support**

It may be that the couple wish to explore particular issues further, or would welcome the assurance that they could ask the group or some of its members for help in times of difficulty. It is often helpful to ask the couple specifically how they would wish such matters to be arranged.

> Young people want something much more than legal clearance or sex education. They see marriage under the care of a meeting, not as the beginning of a relationship, but as the outward recognition of a union that has already reached some permanence and maturity. They want to know how to make it lasting and fulfilling. Are we equal to what they want from us? We will not be if we cannot lay aside our judgmental feelings that right and wrong are matters of rules that are broken or kept. They feel that no words of church or state can make holy a relationship that is not already based on mutual caring. Caring is what matters most to them: caring what happens to your partner, to yourself, to your children, to your friends and family, to human

beings, to the earth. Caring determines whether a relationship is right or wrong. Can we hear what they are saying and asking, and not judge them adversely because their lifestyle is different?

Elizabeth Watson, 1984

Questions for reflection and discussion

1. How obvious is it to members and attenders of our meetings that a meeting for clearness can be made available?

2. Are all couples contemplating making a permanent commitment to one another encouraged to ask for a meeting for clearness?

How do we uphold couples who make a commitment?

Our life is love, and peace, and tenderness; and bearing one with another, and forgiving one another, and not laying accusations one against another; but praying one for another, and helping one another up with a tender hand.

Qfp 10.01

There are various ways in which a couple may make their commitment.

Committed Relationships

Do the couple wish to marry, and if so will it be a civil or Quaker wedding? Do the couple wish to register a civil partnership, and if so do they wish to celebrate their commitment to each other in a meeting for worship?

- The couple may not wish to make a statement of their commitment but trust that Friends will keep it in mind. Overseers will be responsible for their ongoing care and support.

- They may wish to give their commitment a religious dimension through a special meeting for worship (*Qfp* 22.44-46). Elders will be responsible for arranging this.

- We would encourage heterosexual couples to marry one another at this meeting, see *Quaker faith & practice* 1.02.23. If they are free to do so legally, they must include the words set out in *Quaker faith & practice* 16.36-37 in their declarations.

- They may wish to have a civil ceremony, followed by a meeting for worship as suggested in the registering officer's handbook.

- Similarly we would encourage a couple of the same sex to register their civil partnership, and to celebrate that commitment in a Quaker meeting for worship.

In marriage, a private relationship becomes public and thereby receives legitimacy, practical support and blessing from social institutions and the worshipping group.

Qfp 22.33

When there is a Quaker marriage, it is our practice for the couple to sign a certificate of record. Two witnesses sign immediately afterwards (*Qfp* 16.40). Towards the close of the meeting the certificate is read out. After the meeting is over, everyone else signs the certificate as a permanent record of witness. A similar certificate could be drawn up and witnessed where the meeting for commitment is not also a marriage. When the couple have married in meeting, legal forms also have to be completed and signed by them and the registering officer.

As the couple's public commitment will be to a long-term relationship, so the meeting's commitment to them should be seen as long-term and ongoing (see Appendix 3).

Without change there can be no growth: though change may be wanted, welcomed and planned, it will always carry within it some stress and some loss. Something always needs to be let go of in order to move forward. A statement of commitment will change any relationship. It will be a milestone among the many changes as the couple move through the predictable and unpredictable happenings of their life together.

Questions for reflection and discussion

1. How do we encourage the couple to explore the implications of the changes arising from commitment?

2. How do we celebrate their joys and gains?

3. How do we support couples through periods of stress in their relationship?

What is our role if a couple whose relationship is under our care decide to separate?

We do not lightly make public commitments and those made before God and our meeting bind tightly. Yet, despite their and our best efforts, a couple in a committed relationship can sometimes break apart. This applies equally to a marriage or any other lifelong commitment. Each person may feel grief and guilt, even when no one else is involved. Each must come to terms with the failure of expectations – theirs and ours – and with being single again. It is important that the couple are encouraged (perhaps through a meeting for clearness) to consider the wider implications, particularly when children are involved.

Meetings are encouraged to give further consideration to the issues surrounding breakdown of relationships, separation and divorce.

Love is affection and friendship; caring and sharing; creative and joyful; giving, receiving and forgiving. It is the acceptance of all aspects of our nature, including our creativity, our intellect, our various faults and abilities, our colour, our sex and our sexuality. When we learn how to love, we learn also how to worship.

We are none of us perfect, and none of us achieves perfection in our relationships. We know only too well that we are often hurtful or exploitive, and say things that we afterwards bitterly regret. But we know that we can be forgiven, and that, through our good experiences of love, we are enabled to hear those promptings of love and truth in our hearts through which we can catch a glimpse of the right way forward.

Quaker Home Service, 1988

There are three things that last forever; faith, hope and love; and the greatest of the three is love.

1 Corinthians 13.13

Appendix 1

Civil Partnership Act

The Civil Partnership Act, that came into force in
December 2005, enables same sex couples to register
their partnerships via their local registry office. The
process is similar to civil marriage and confers the same
legal, financial and inheritance rights that have previously
been reserved to heterosexual couples.

Civil partnership registration is a purely secular process;
registrars cannot include Quaker meeting houses, or
any other building with religious associations, among the
approved venues. Quaker registering officers are not
licensed to undertake these registrations; they are only
permitted to register Quaker marriages. Nor is it legally
possible to use the word 'marriage' on any certificate
that might be created to record a celebration of such a
commitment.

This continuing lack of equal status in law is a matter that
concerns many Friends. They do not wish to imply any
difference in value or status of any relationships be they
same-sex or heterosexual*. Many would wish to be able

---

* This issue was bought in 2006 to Meeting for Sufferings, which is
consulting Friends and meetings on the way forward. For information
on developments, contact the Assistant Recording Clerk, at Friends
House.

to offer same-sex couples a legally appointed meeting for worship, just as they do for heterosexual couples.

For more information on civil partnership registration contact your local Register Office or go to the website of the General Register Office at

www.gro.gov.uk/gro/content/civilpartnerships

At the time of writing (early 2006) most Friends undertaking civil partnership registrations have been in a committed relationship for a considerable time – some even for 40 or 50 years. For these couples this ceremony is a public celebration with legal status conferred as a result, a step many would have taken earlier if not prevented. Many of these Friends have already celebrated their commitment to each other in a Quaker meeting for worship.

Quaker meetings have been quick to respond with support for Friends undertaking registration and some have helped the couple celebrate by arranging a special meeting for worship.

Preparation for such meetings for worship needs to be carefully considered with those responsible for eldership within the meeting, to take into account the status of the relationship (long established or relatively new), the composition of the meeting (some Friends may strongly disapprove) and the wishes of the couple. In some instances a meeting for commitment may be appropriate, in others a meeting of celebration. We also need to remember that our meetings for worship are normally open to anyone to attend.

As the meeting for worship has no legal standing its form is at the discretion of Friends. The couple may wish to make or re-make a declaration of intention and have a certificate of record signed by those present similar to that outlined in *Qfp* 16.36-40. It is also normal for meetings to record, by minute, significant events in the life of the Quaker community.

No doubt in time we will accumulate sufficient experience of such meetings that a pattern of preferred practice will emerge that we will add to our writings.

Appendix 2

This is the text of the leaflet produced by one preparative meeting.

Are you thinking about a meeting for commitment?

You may feel that you would like to express your commitment to your partner in a Quaker meeting. Some couples may wish to marry in a meeting for worship. Those who may not marry there (perhaps because they are of the same gender) may nevertheless want to recognise a spiritual dimension to their relationship. Sometimes couples who are already married may want to renew their commitment to each other. A meeting for commitment can be arranged for all of these.

Who can have a meeting for commitment?

Meetings for worship are probably the most distinctive feature of a community of the Religious Society of Friends (Quakers). A Quaker meeting for commitment is a meeting for worship for a special occasion. Members of the meeting and attenders (people who come to meeting for worship on a regular basis) may ask for such a meeting.

What is a meeting for commitment?

The simple Quaker meeting where the couple, together with friends and members of the meeting, gather in worship is for Friends the most natural setting for the two of you to make a commitment to each other in the presence of God. With your declaration you take each other freely and equally as life-long partners, committing yourselves to joining your lives in loving companionship, asking God's blessing on your union. You believe that, whatever stresses and strains may arise in the relationship, these can be resolved if both partners are able and filling to trust each other in a generous spirit. With God's help your love for each other can deepen and change in a lifetime together. Those who attend the meeting are not present merely as witnesses; they accept the responsibility to uphold both of you throughout your life together by their prayers, friendship and practical assistance.

How can we be sure we are doing the right thing?

Do you both want to make this commitment to one another in the presence of God and to the meeting? This is the vital question. To help you answer it, the first step may be to arrange a meeting for clearness. This meeting consists of three or four Friends or attenders of your choice, who meet with the two of you in worship to work out if you are both clear about what you are planning to do. Are you clear of other commitments? Is your relationship clearly founded? Do you both want public and religious recognition of your commitment?

A meeting for clearness is not an interrogation. It can be a wonderful experience, like being visited for membership. Finding clearness can be a relief and a joy. For those who do not feel that a meeting for clearness is right for them, elders will discuss their request and try to help them find the right way forward.

How do we arrange for a meeting for commitment?

If all feel the way is clear, your next step will be to approach an elder to make arrangements for a special meeting for worship to celebrate your commitment to one another.

If you and your partner are single and of opposite genders, you can also marry one another in meeting (see *Quaker faith & practice,* chapter 16). You should arrange to talk with the Quaker registering officer as soon as possible to ensure that the requirements of the law and of the Religious Society of Friends are completed in time. This may take up to three months.

What happens in a meeting for commitment?

One of the essential characteristics of a Quaker meeting is its simplicity. If you wish to wear something smart and give one another rings, you may do so. However, what is important is that at the meeting you both commit yourselves to one another in the presence of God.

The meeting begins when the first person enters the room, and by the time appointed everyone should be present and sitting in silent worship. As the procedure may not be familiar to all of your guests, you should arrange for an experienced Friend to stand soon after the meeting begins and give a welcome and a brief explanation of what is to follow. Then there is a period of silence. When you are both ready, you stand, take each other by the hand, and declare your commitment to one another. You may then sign a certificate of record and two witnesses may sign immediately afterwards.

If this is also a marriage, you **have** to include prescribed words in your declaration. Details are set out in *Quaker faith & practice* chapter 16. Quaker weddings have been conducted since the 17th century and are the subject of special Acts of Parliament. The couple, the registering officer and the two witnesses also have to complete the official register.

This is followed by a period of silent shared worship during which anyone present may stand and speak. People may express their love and support for you in whatever words they find most natural. If they feel that it would contribute to the spirit of worship, they may ask for God's blessing on your commitment and offer their prayers for you. The meeting usually lasts about forty minutes – the end is indicated when the elders for the meeting shake hands. Everyone else may shake hands with their neighbours.

Towards the close of the meeting the certificate of commitment is read out. After the meeting is over, everyone else signs the certificate as a permanent record of witness.

Appendix 3

Committing in the care of the meeting

When a declaration of commitment is witnessed by a meeting, the meeting takes a responsibility to uphold it. The commitment is 'in the care of the meeting', in addition to the oversight of the two individuals. We can offer support in our prayers; we also need to consider the practical and emotional support which will not only sustain at the time of making the commitment but will be helpful and enabling to the couple as they deal with changes in the future.

The essence of a wedding or meeting for commitment is a declaration in public, before the whole meeting (or representatives of that meeting) and friends and family. The couple must have made a strong commitment personally to each other, to have reached this stage. The meeting for worship is one step in a long process, a life-long, developing relationship. It is the stage where the relationship becomes formal, public, and the wider circle of people concerned indicate their involvement. Legal and financial arrangements are generally part of the package called marriage (for heterosexual couples), or civil partnership registration (for same sex couples), and they are another link for the couple, a support when needed.

The certificate is a record of witness, and witness, as we know from our Testimonies, implies a living responsibility.

But how do we as Friends, as a Quaker community, do that caring? We often have good intentions but is there a framework that reminds us to carry out these intentions?

A clearness meeting is probably the best foundation for continued support for the couple, so that several people (not just the registering officer) have a good basis of openness, trust, sensitivity and care. For how a clearness meeting for marriage or commitment works, see page 16 and the publications list at the end of this book.

As individuals, show that you mean what you say about continuing to care.

- You could invite the couple to supper a few weeks after the meeting for commitment or wedding. The occasion might offer the fun of looking at the photographs but the couple will appreciate that your support and friendship can be depended on.

- Perhaps you could arrange a reunion of the clearness group a year after the first clearness meeting. It could be a celebration or another clearness meeting – at its best it is a friendly occasion when people can move naturally into worship, celebration, openness, whatever feels right. You might put this date in everyone's diary at the first clearness meeting and end the reunion by talking about the following year's reunion.

- Send a card to mark the completion of their first year.

- Look out for suitable events at Woodbrooke and other Quaker places.

- A special gift would be a weekend away to spend time, with each other – e.g. a weekend of child care, money for the train fare, whatever is appropriate, about the time of their first anniversary.

Appendix 4

Suggested questions to be raised with couples contemplating making a commitment to each other under the care of the meeting

- Are you seeking a spiritual union, a legal union, or both?

- If you do not seek a legal union, have you taken the necessary steps to compensate for this? Are you legally free of other binding relationships? Have you taken steps to prepare for wills and other legal documents?

- What are your expectations of your relationship/ marriage? What does the public commitment of your relationship in meeting for worship mean to you? What are your understandings of the spiritual and corporate nature of a Quaker marriage/meeting for commitment?

- What do you think about the traditional masculine and feminine roles? Can you both see yourselves moving comfortably between different roles – for example, home-making and wage earning, as the need arises?

- Why do you think you will make good partners? Are you able to compromise your plans and wishes out of respect to one another? Are you able to talk comfortably about feelings to one another? Do you know your own, and your partner's strengths and weaknesses – and do you agree with each other's perceptions? What things are fun to do together? Can you laugh at yourself, and with your partner? How do you deal with conflicts between you?

- How are you financing your life together? Who will pay for housekeeping necessities, education, recreation, medical needs, etc?

- Have you thoroughly discussed any health problems, both physical and mental, you have had or might have?

- How do you feel about each other's families? Do you enjoy each other's friends? Can you have personal relationships that do not include your partner?

- Are you willing to give time, patience and openness to a good sexual relationship? What do you feel about sexual and emotional fidelity?

- Are you aware that a committed relationship needs constant care, nurture and communication to ensure good growth? Are you willing to recommit yourselves, day by day and year by year, to persevere in spite of difficulties and disagreements; to recognise, accept, love and delight in each other's individuality?

- If appropriate, have you discussed the possibility of having children or stepchildren, and considered the issues – physical, emotional, moral, financial – that such a change will bring?

Adapted, with thanks, from *Marriage Queries for Lesbian, Gay and Straight Couples* – Putney Friends Meeting 1993

Appendix 5 Publications

The Quaker Bookshop and mail order.

For current prices and availability of specific titles, and a general mail order catalogue, including *Quaker faith & practice* and the *Book of Meetings*, contact the Quaker Bookshop in London.

You can buy books in person from the Quaker Bookshop, or by mail order, by post, over the telephone on 0207 663 1030, or visit the website, www.quaker.org.uk and click on bookshop.

Some books may be out of print but are of historic interest; they may be found in meeting house libraries or borrowed from the Quaker Life Resources Room at Friends House. Contact the Library of Britain Yearly Meeting for minutes and other reference materials.

Out of print

Although this book, *Committed Relationships,* focuses on lifelong steadfast commitment, some publications on sexuality and on separation and divorce are also included here. Titles with a strong Quaker content are listed. Excellent and comprehensive lists of other publications are available from organisations in Appendix 6.

Quaker faith & practice, third edition 2005. The book of Christian discipline of the Yearly Meeting of the Religious Society of Friends (Quakers) in Britain.

The book of meetings. New edition each February listing contact details of every Quaker meeting and organisation in Britain.

Earlham School of Religion, ***Among Friends***, Earlham Press, 1999. A consultation with Friends about the condition of Quakers in the United States today.

McBee, Patricia, ed. ***Grounded in God: Care and Nurture in Friends Meetings,*** Quaker Press of Friends general Conference, 2002 has several chapters on marriage, commitment, support, divorce, being single or in a family: an essential resource for all meetings.

Family Life Sub-Committee, ***Living with oneself and others.*** New England YM, Committee on Ministry and Counsel, 1993. The varied chapters for those contemplating marriage, living without a partner, facing old age or death, considering parenthood, etc, centre round queries for private reflection or for a clearness meeting. Some sets of queries are for the meeting as a whole to consider. These queries exemplify well the prayerful, seeking, non-judgmental yet honest process of a clearness meeting, as well as offering a way for a meeting as a whole to consider important matters of principle.

Family Relations Committee, *A resource guide to be used by a same-sex couple*, Philadelphia YM, 1988. Acknowledges divided judgments of Friends while honouring all couples. Includes advices, queries and bibliography.

Family Relations Committee, *A Quaker marriage.* Philadelphia Yearly Meeting. Their basic booklet: information, questions, queries and advice for the couple, for the committee on clearness and for the committee on oversight, covering preparation for marriage, the wedding, and support afterwards. The legal context is Pennsylvanian, but the description of 'marriage in the care of the meeting' is thoughtful and helpful.

Green, T and Woodrow, P, *Insight and action: How to discover and support a life of integrity and commitment to change.* New Society Publishers. Philadelphia, PA, 1994. Arising out of experience in communities with a concern for peace and justice, there is extremely useful and straightforward material on support groups, clearness for individual decision making, strategic

questioning, group processes, and sections quoted
from books of discipline and the Quaker consultation on
discernment.

Hill, Leslie, *Marriage: a spiritual leading for lesbian,
gay and straight couples,* Pendle Hill Pamphlet 308,
1993. When George Fox and Margaret Fell married, theirs
was a testimony to equality, independence and respect
for the value of each person's calling and service to God,
What is the meaning and purpose of marriage, today?

Hoffman, Jan, *Clearness committees and their use in
personal discernment and Clearness committees,
committees of care and committees of oversight,*
from Organisation and Procedure of Canadian Yearly
Meeting, 1990. This and other informative sheets can
be found in **Fostering vital Friends meetings.** Part 2
can be obtained from http://www.fgcquaker.org/library/
fosteringmeetings/fosvi2.pdf

Loring, Patricia, *Listening spirituality.* Volumes 1 and 2,
Openings Press, Maryland, Vol 1: 1997. Volume 2: 1999.
Volume 1 on personal spiritual practice among Friends
and Volume 2 on corporate practices include sections on
spiritual guidance, clearness and discernment set in their
fundamental context, as part of a whole way of life.

Loring, Patricia, *Spiritual discernment,* Pendle Hill
Pamphlet 305, 1992. The context and goal of clearness
committees: 'it is tempting to prepare check-lists... it's

best that awareness of all these elements be part of the preparation, then let go of... under the guidance of the Spirit'.

Milligan, Edward H. *Quaker Marriage,* Quaker Tapestry Booklets 1994. A simple, readable account of Quaker marriage in Britain and Ireland in the last 350 years.

Peck, M Scott, *The road less travelled.* Arrow Books. 1990.

The recognition of same-sex relationships in the Religious Society of Friends. Study pack compiled by the same-sex relationship group of Meeting for Sufferings, London Yearly Meeting, Quaker Home Service, 1988. A collection of minutes, discussion papers and records of discussions in Quaker groups, to help in their consideration.

Sawtell, Roger and Susan, *Reflections from a Long Marriage.* Swarthmore Lecture 2006, Quaker Books. An ecumenical couple, working in co-operatives, living in a community, explore their marriage, 'where the energy of the two together is greater than they have separately'.

The Revised English Bible, Oxford University Press and Cambridge University Press, 1989.

Sexuality and human relationships, Quaker Social Responsibility & Education, 1983. An interim report on a project in London Yearly Meeting, 1979 – 1983, and the experience of meetings that considered these topics.

Speaking our truth: plain Quaker's guide to lesbian and gay lives, Quaker Lesbian and Gay Fellowship, 1993.

Watson, Elizabeth, *Marriage in the Light,* 1993 Philadelphia YM. Useful, perceptive, inspiring, readable.

When the wind changes: young people's experiences of divorce and changing family patterns. Divorce & changing family patterns project of Children & Young People's Committee, Quaker Home Service, 2001. 'Divorce is a bit of a dodgy one...' 'Having two homes comes with pros and cons...' 'What is 'normal' anyway?'

Who do we think we are? Young friends' commitment and belonging. Young Friends General Meeting, the 1998 Swarthmore Lecture, QHS. Contrasts, assertions, perplexities and poetic arguments!

Friends Journal

Most monthly meetings have, in one of their local meeting libraries, sets of **Quaker Monthly** or **The Friend** with many relevant articles; the periodicals of other Quaker yearly meetings will also contain many useful articles. Here we list a few from the **Friends Journal**. The Quaker Bookshop sells current issues. Visitors can refer to bound volumes in the Library of Britain Yearly Meeting at Friends House. A photocopy of an article can be made for personal research – contact the Library for information.

Bacon, Margaret Hope, *Grow old along with me*, 1994 February. A support group of couples married at least 45 years finds that even 'if it ain't broke' it can be made better.

Bacon, Margaret Hope, *Sharing work and faith,* 1993 January. The marriage of Lucretia and James Mott. 'When Lucretia Matt was present at a marriage she liked to make a statement: in the true married relationship, the independence of husband and wife will be equal, their dependence mutual, and their obligations reciprocal.'

Baker, Judith, *Friendly divorce,* 1995 June. 'If we can let go of judgment, spiritual growth for both the family and the meeting can be the result.'

Barber, Laurence, *The marriage question(s),* 1994 January, 'Should the meeting be merely content to set unions afloat... or do Friends have responsibility to avoid shipwreck?'

Griscom Betsy, *A meeting for worship with a concern for divorce.* 1998 April. 'It is clear to me that the process of preparing for the meeting for worship with a concern for divorce, and the worship itself, have turned my divorce from an experience of rejection and loss into an act of acceptance, love and growth.'

Kelly, Arlene, *Separation and divorce,* 1991 February. 'It is the spirit working which will ultimately bring openings and healing.'

Kolodny, Debra and Renshaw, Betty, *As long as we both shall live,* 1994 February. One meeting's path to a same-gender marriage minute.

McBee, Patricia *Marriage as a spiritual discipline,* 1994 July. 'By engaging in a discipline of time and listening and faith and love, we found an outcome that allowed each of us to feel more loved, more deeply understood, and more free to grow.'

Post, Stephen, *Marriage vows,* 1993 February. Reflecting on the words of his promise.

Segal, Rima, *Some questions concerning marriage,* 1990 August. 'Marriage, being a lifelong union of spiritual as well as temporal interests, presents considerations of vital importance to Friends.'

Appendix 6 Organisations

The address for all the central offices and services of
Britain Yearly Meeting of the Religious Society of Friends
(Quakers) in Britain (BYM) is:

Friends House
173 Euston Road
London NW1 2BJ
England
Telephone switchboard: +44 (0) 20 7663 1000
Fax; +44 (0) 20 7663 1001 Website: www.quaker.org.uk

Particular departments can also be contacted directly:

The Committee on Eldership & Oversight and **The
Quaker Life Resources Room**
Telephone: +44 (0) 20 7663 1023
E-mail: anneh@quaker.org.uk

The Quaker Bookshop (for information on all Quaker
publications)
Telephone: +44 (0) 20 7663 1030/1031
E-mail: bookshop@quaker.org.uk

Methodist Publishing House (for 'Quaker books' mail order)
MPH
4 John Wesley Road
Werrington
Peterborough PE4 6ZP
England
Telephone switchboard: +44 (0) 1733 325 002
Fax; +44 (0) 01733 384 180
Website: www,mph.org.uk
email: sales@mph.org.uk

Retreats and Courses

You may find suitable events such as couples enrichment listed in current programmes of retreats and courses. A full address list of Quaker study and conference centres and retreat houses in Britain can be found in the current *Book of meetings* and on the Britain Yearly Meeting website.

Or contact:

Woodbrooke Quaker Study Centre
1046 Bristol Road Birmingham B29 6LJ
Telephone: +44 (0) 121 472 5171
Fax: +44(0) 121 472 5173
Web: www.woodbrooke.org.uk
email: enquiries@woodbrookc.org.uk

Quaker Lesbian & Gay Fellowship
For support and information about events and publications, see the current *Book of Meetings* for the name and address of the contact person.

Stonewall
Tower Building
York Road
London SE1 7NX
Telephone: +44 (0) 020 7593 1850
Fax: +44(0) 020 7593 1877
Minicom: +44(0) 020 7633 0759
E-mail: info@stonewall.org.uk
Stonewall campaigns for equality and justice for Lesbians, Gay Men and Bisexuals, and offers much useful information. You can download their guide to civil partnerships, *Get Hitched,* also in large print or various languages from
www.stonewall.org.uk/information_bank/partnership

Lesbian and Gay Christian Movement
Oxford House
Derbyshire Street
London E2 6HG
Phone/fax: 020 7739 31249
Helpline: 020 7739 8134
E-mail: lgcm@aol.com
Website: www.lgcm.org.uk
Information, advice, journal booklists.

Friends Journal to subscribe or buy back issues:
1216 Arch Street, 2A
Philadelphia
PA 19107-2835
USA
Telephone: 001 215 563-8629
Fax: 001 215 568-1377
E-mail: info@friendsjournal.org
Website: www.friendsjournal.org

The Association for Marriage Enrichment 'Focus on
Couples'. To participate in weekend courses receive a
newsletter or join a local group of couples, go to
www.ame-uk.org.uk

Relate (formerly National Marriage Guidance) For
counselling and education for marriage and personal
relationships, look in your local telephone directory for
your nearest branch, or visit: www, relate.org.uk where
you can buy Relate publications.
Telephone: + 44 (0) 1788 563816
E-mail; bookshop@national.relate.org.uk

www.ingramcontent.com/pod-product-compliance
Lightning Source LLC
Chambersburg PA
CBHW022344040426
42449CB00006B/710